THE KORAN

[in 21 pages]

Auther mee

[ZHINGOORA BOOKS]

This digital edition is published by Zhingoora Books.

The Cover is Designed by Pallav Sethiya.

zhingoora_books@yahoo.com

THE KORAN

The Koran, the sacred book of Islam, and of more than a hundred millions of men, is the least original of all existing sacred books. Muslims agree in believing that it is from beginning to end, and word for word, inspired; and that it existed before the Creation on what is called the "Preserved Tablet." This tablet was brought by the Archangel Gabriel from the highest to the lowest heaven, whence it was dictated sura [chapter] by sura, verse by verse, and word by word, to the Prophet Muhammad. Its matter is, however, taken for the most part from the Old Testament, especially the narrative portions of the Pentateuch; from the New Testament; from the traditions of the ancient Arabs; and also from Zoroastrian and other scriptures or traditions. It is not likely that Muhammad used literary sources, except in a small measure. But there were Jews, Christians, Zoroastrians, and others in and around Arabia, and he must have learned from their lips the principal doctrines of their respective religions. Nevertheless, planless and fragmentary compilation though it be, the Koran, particularly in the earlier suras written at Mekka, has much of the grandeur and poetry of style and the passionate exaltation of a true prophet, the sincerity of whose zeal is unquestioned.

Introductory

The word "Koran," or "Quran,"[13] from a root qara = to read, means literally "what is to be read," i.e., the written authority on all matters, religions, etc. It is the exact equivalent of the Rabbinical Hebrew word "Miqra" (from the Hebrew qara = to read). The idea involved in both the Arabic and Hebrew words is that what is so designated is the ultimate authority deciding all questions. The Rabbis of post-Biblical times (compare the Jewish Qabbalah) regarded the Old Testament as an encyclopaedia of universal knowledge. In the best-knownMuslim universities of modern times philosophy, science, and everything else are taught from the Koran, which is made in some way to contain implicitly the latest words of modern thought, invention, and discovery.

The Koran did not exist as a whole until after the Prophet Muhammad's[14] death. It was then compiled by the order of Abu Bekr, the first Sunnite Caliph. Its contents were found written on palm leaves white stones, and other articles capable of being written on. The compilers depended, to a large extent, upon the memory of the prophet's first followers, but the Koran, as we now have it, existed without any appreciable divergence by the end of the first year, after Muhammad's death (A.D. 632).

This Muslim Bible has no scheme or plan because it is an almost haphazard compilation of unconnected discourses, uttered on various unexplained occasions, and dealing with many incidents and themes. There is practically no editing, and no attempt is made to explain when, or how, or why the various speeches were delivered.

The earliest native writers and commentators on the Koran arranged its suras in two main classes: (1) Those uttered at Mekka before the flight in A.D. 622; (2) those written at Medinah during the next ten years.

Most recent scholars follow the chronological arrangement proposed by the great Orientalist Nöldeke in 1860. Friedrich Schwally in his newly revised edition of Nöldeke's great work on the Koran follows his master in almost every detail. Rodwell's translation of the Koran, recently issued in "Everyman's Library," arranges the suras chronologically according to Nöldeke'sscheme. In the summaries that follow, it is this chronological order that is adopted. In the Arabic editions followed by the well-known and valuable translations of Sale, E.H. Palmer (Clarendon Press, "Sacred Books of the East," vols. 6 and 9), and others, the principle adopted is to put the longest suras first and the shortest last.

The Mekkan suras are much more original than the Medinah ones, especially those of the first period--*i.e.*, those belonging to the first four years of Muhammad's prophetic mission, *e.g.*, suras 96, 74, etc. In these suras the style is grander, more passionate, and fuller of poetry. The prophet appears in a state of great mental exaltation, full of a zeal which no words can adequately express, and of a sincerity which few scholars have questioned.

The suras of the second period, the following two years of the prophet's mission (*e.g.*, suras 54, 37, etc.), have the same general character, but are less vehement. Still less vehement and more restrained are the suras of the third Mekkan period--*i.e.*, from the seventh year of the prophet's mission to his flight in A.D. 622 (*e.g.*, suras 32, 41, etc.). The style of the Medinah suras resembles that of the Mekkan revelations of the third period, only they are still more matter of fact and restrained, and are largely made up of appeals to Jews, Christians, and others to abandon their "unbelief," and to accept the prophet who had come to them with the true religion, a religion as old as Abraham, though forgotten for many ages.

The Koran differs from the Scriptures of the Old and New Testaments, including the Apocrypha, in that these latter are much-more varied, as emanating from many minds, and belonging to very different occasions. The Koran is, from beginning to end, the effusions (often very wild) of one man.

The present editor has kept before him the Arabic text of Maracci, Fluegel, and Redslob, and also severalOriental editions (Cairo, Constantinople, Calcutta, etc.). But, of course, the best known translations, and also the native commentaries (Baidhawi, etc.), have been consulted.

In the summaries which follow, numerals following the paragraphs indicate the number of the sura or suras in the Arabic text as well as in Sale's translation.

MEKKAN SURAS

I.--FIRST PERIOD (A.D. 613-617)

Muhammad's First Call to Read the Koran

In the name of the gracious and compassionate God.[15]

Recite in the name of thy Lord, who created man and taught men to write, recite what God has revealed to thee His Prophet, and be not afraid. Consider not the opposition of Abu Gahl, who has threatened to put his foot on thy neck if thou dost worship Allah. (96.)

Denunciation of Abu Lahab[16]

Abu Lahab's two hands shall perish, and he himself shall perish. His wealth shall not avail him, nor all that he has gained. He shall be burnt in the fiery flames[17] of Hell, his wife carrying wood for fuel, with a cord of palm-tree fibres twisted round her neck. (III.)

Muhammad Commanded to Offer Sacrifices

We have given to thee, O Prophet, great wealth and abounding riches. Pray thou to Allah, and offer Him suitable sacrifices out of what He has bestowed upon thee. (108.)

[Compare with this paragraph the following, from sura 22 of the Medinah group:

We have ordained that ye offer sacrifices unto Allah, and that ye receive much benefit therefrom. When, therefore, ye slay your camels let the name of Allah be pronounced over them. Then eat of them and give to those who ask humbly, giving also to the poor and needy who ask not. Flesh and blood can never reach unto Allah (God), but your obedience and piety will reach unto Him.]

Believers and Unbelievers

We will make the path to happiness easy and safe to all such as fear Allah, and give alms, and believe the truth proclaimed by Allah's messenger. But we will make easy the path to distress and misery for all such as are niggardly, are bent on making riches, and deny the truth when it is proclaimed to them. When these last fall headlong into Hell, their wealth will avail them nothing. In the burning furnace they shall burn and broil. (92.)

The Duty of Exercising Charity

Verily, We (God) have created some men in such poverty and distress as to need the help of others. What does that braggart man mean when he says, "None shall prevail over me; I have and have scattered riches boundless"? Does he not know that there is a Divine eye that sees him? Have not We created him with a capacity of distinguishing between the two highways, that which descends towards evil, and that which ascends towards thegood? This niggardly man, however, makes no attempt to scale the heights. What is it to ascend the upward road? It is to free the prisoner, to feed the hungry, to defend the orphan who is akin, and the down-trodden poor. Besides this, it is enjoined that men believe in Allah and His Prophet; that they encourage each other to be steadfast in the faith, exercising mutual consideration and sympathy. All such as do these things shall be the people of the right hand. But all those who disbelieve Our signs shall be the companions of the left hand, over whom shall be a vault of fire. (90.)

Muhammad Commanded to Arise and Preach

O thou mantle-wrapped one, arise and warn the people, and magnify the Lord. The Day of Judgment will be a sad day for unbelievers. Leave thou thine enemy in Mine hands, and let Me visit upon him his well deserved punishment. For he has ridiculed the Koran; he has said: "This is nothing else than magic, they are the words of a man." I [God] will cast him into Hell, where he shall burn in torment. The fires of this Hell leave nothing unconsumed. It scorches men's flesh. We have appointed nineteen angels as guardians over Hell fire. But why nineteen? That believers may be sure of the veracity of this Book, and that unbelievers may have occasion for denying the divinity of the Koran, saying: "What means this number?" (74.)

The Koran Given to Muhammad

Verily, We have brought down to Muhammad the Koran on the Night of Power.[18] This one Night of Power is better than a thousand months. On that night did Gabriel and the angels descend and reveal to Our Prophetall the words of the Koran. (97.)

Muhammad not Mad nor an Impostor

Believe thou not, O Messenger of Mine, when they say, "Thou art bereft of thy senses," when they charge thee with imposture. Thy Lord knoweth who are bereft of their senses, and who are the impostors. Warn thou those maligners of the awful judgment which awaits them. (68.)

God's Promise to Help Muhammad to Recite the Koran

We [Allah] shall enable thee to remember all the parts of the Koran, so that thou mayest recite them for the encouragement of those who believe and as a warning to all unbelievers. Nor shalt thou forget aught of this Revelation except what We please.[19] All those who fear God will receive the prophet's warning, but all those who disbelieve shall be cast into terrible fire where they will neither live nor die. This doctrine which We command thee to preach is that taught in the ancient Books, the Books of Abraham and of Moses, who were faithful Muslims. (87.)

The Koran Inspired

By the falling star, your comrade Muhammad does not err, nor does he speak his own mind. What he utters has been revealed to him. The Koran is from God through Gabriel; it is not the work of man. Why worship ye goddesses like Allat and Al'Uzza and Manah?There are no goddesses.[20] (53.)

The Treatment of Women Believers

When believing women come to you as fugitives, leaving behind them unbelieving husbands, send them not back to the infidels, but test their faith, and if they are found true Muslims, pay back to their husbands the dowries which they have expended. Then may ye marry them, provided ye give them the accustomed dowries. (60.)

God's Unity[21]

Say "He is but one God, the everlasting God who begets not,[22] nor is begotten, and there is none like unto Him." (10.)

Formulæ of Exorcism

I flee for refuge to the Lord, that He may protect me against the evil things which He has created. Against night goblins when the night comes on, and from witches who bind by their magic knots, and from such as injure by the evil eye; I seek refuge with the Lord from charmers, from jinns [demons], and from evil men. (113.)

[pg 177]

The Heaven of the Muslims

All who believe in Allah and His Prophet shall be admitted hereafter into delightful gardens [Paradise]. They shall repose for ever on couches decked with gold and precious stones, being supplied with abundance of luscious wine, fruits of the choicest variety, and the flesh of birds. They shall be accompanied by damsels of unsurpassed beauty, with large black, pearl-like eyes. (56.)

II.--SECOND PERIOD (A.D. 617-619)

Winds and Demons Subject to Solomon

And We made a strong wind subject to Solomon, so that it conveyed him whither he would. We also gave him the power of commanding demons, so that they dived into the sea to bring him pearls, and did everything else that he wished.[23] (21.)

The Miraculous Birth of Jesus

Remember Mary, who preserved her virginity, and into whom We breathed Our own spirit, so that when her son Isa [Jesus] was born, mother and son became a sign unto all mankind. (21.)

The Virgin Mary

After Mary, the Virgin, had begotten her son Isa [Jesus] she was found one day carrying the child in her arms when some pious men met her and rebuked her, saying: "O Mary, thou sister of Aaron,[24] what is thisstrange thing thou hast done? Thy father

Amram was an upright man, and thy mother was no harlot, as thou seemest to be." In answer to all this the infant child, not having previously lisped a syllable, said, "Verily, I am the servant of Allah, who has given me the Book of the Gospel, and appointed me to be His Prophet. He has made me blessed, and to be a blessing. Happy the day wherein I was born, and the day wherein I shall die, and the day whereon I shall be raised again." (19.)

Devils Sent by God to Make Men Sin

De ye not know that We [God] send devils against the unbelievers to move them, by their suggestions, to the sin of which these unbelievers become guilty? (19.)

Solomon's Army of Men, Birds, and Jinns (Demons)

Solomon was able to understand the speech of birds and to make them understand his speech.[25] There gathered to him on a certain day his entire army of men, birds, and jinns in the Valley of Ants. The crowd was so great that one of the ants said to his fellows, "Get you at once into your ant-homes, or you will be trampled to death by one of these myriad feet."

The Queen of Sheba's Visit to Solomon

Solomon, one day reviewing his varied troops, missed among the birds the hoopoe, and asked whither this bird had gone, threatening all manner of punishments for his absence. Soon the missing bird came flying to the king, uttering the words, "I have just come from Sheba, where I have looked upon the most wonderful queen, sitting upon the most magnificent throne that I have ever set eyes on. But this queen and her subjects, unfortunately, worshipped not Allah, the true God, but the sun."

"I will test the truth of thy words!" replied the angry monarch. "Take thou this note of mine to the queen thou laudest so highly, bidding her come to my kingdom to acknowledge my authority."

Almost in a twinkling the hoopoe was back with the queen's answer consenting to visit Solomon and his dominions. Solomon, having received this answer, asked the nobles of his kingdom, "Which of you will bring me at once the Queen of Sheba's throne, to be here before she arrives?"

"I will!" said one of the wickedest of the jinns.

"And so will I, in a whiff!" answered a jinn that was well acquainted with the Scriptures.

In a very short time the throne was in Solomon's palace. "Alter ye it," said the king, "as much as ye may, to see whether she has any supernatural knowledge to identify it."

When the queen arrived, she was asked, "What throne is this?"

She replied, "It is mine--strangely mine." After she had witnessed the glory and wisdom of Solomon, she gave up her idols, and became the worshipper of Allah, the true God. (27.)

III.--THIRD PERIOD (A.D. 619-622)

Punishment for Violating the Sabbath

Ye know how We tested and proved those wicked people who dwelt in Elath on the Red Sea. On the Sabbath day We made the fish come right up to them, as if asking to be caught; but not so on other days. Those who yielded to the temptation, and thus violated the sanctity of the sacred day, We turned into apes as a punishment for their wrong-doing. (7.)

Mount Sinai Shaken Above the Israelites

When the Israelites doubted the authority of the Law which We had given them through Moses, Our servant, We caused Mount Sinai to rear itself above them as a covering, so that the people feared it was going to fall upon them. And We said to them, "Receive ye with reverence that Law which We have given you, and remember what is contained therein, taking heed thereto."[26] (7.)

MEDINAH SURAS

Salvation for Others than Muslims

All such as believe in Allah and in the last day, and who do that which is right, whether they are Jews, Christians, Sabeans, or Muslims, shall have their reward from Allah, who will take away from them all fear and grief. (3.)

Muslims Only to be Saved

No one that follows any other religion than Islam will be accepted by God or saved from perishing in the life that is to come. (2.)

Abraham, Ishmael, Isaac, Jacob, and the Tribes of Israel all Muslims

Do ye Jews say that Abraham, Ishmael, Isaac, Jacob, and the tribes of Israel were Jews, or do ye Christians say that they were Christians? But God knows better, and has revealed to you the truth that all these were Muslims, followers of the religion of Islam. But God is cognisant of your unbelief, and will bring you to account. (2.)

The Qiblah Changed from Jerusalem to Mekka

Foolish men will say, "Why have they changed the Qiblah[27] from Jerusalem to the Kaabah[28] in Mekka?" Say to them, "God's is the east and the west, and He has commanded us to turn our face, when we pray, to the sacred mosque at Mekka." (2.)

Against Jews and Christians, Who Capriciously Choose and Reject What Divine Revelations They Please

Why, then, do ye believe part only of the Book, and deny that part which authenticates the mission of the [pg 182]Prophet of Allah? All those who are guilty of this sinshall have shame in this life, and on the Resurrection Day shall be driven into the most excrutiating torments. (2.)

The Mekka Temple Founded by Abraham

It was Abraham, our father, who first entered the Kaabah sanctuary at Mekka, and it is our bounden duty, if at all able, to visit this sacred house. (3.)

Jesus Predicts the Coming of Muhammad

Jesus, Mary's Son, said, "O Israelites, I am Allah's Apostle, sent to confirm the Law of the Old Testament, and to bring you good tidings of a great Apostle to come after me, whose name is Ahmad."[29] (61.)

Muhammad the Last and Greatest of God's Messengers

In the former times We sent Our apostles with convincing arguments and all decisive miracles, and We gave them the Scriptures. We sent to men Noah, Abraham, and the prophets, but many believed not. Then We sent Our apostles, after whom came Jesus, Son of Mary. Then, last of all, came Our great apostle, Muhammad. O all ye believers, fear God and obey the words of Allah's messenger. (57.)

The Koran Consistent Throughout

Why do they not carefully and impartially consider the Koran? If it had not been wholly of God, unbelievers would have been able to find out contradictions. (4.)

Muhammad Contradicts the Fact of the Crucifixion of Christ

Christians say that Christ Jesus, Son of Mary, was slain. But He was not slain, nor crucified, but another was taken for Him. The true Isa [Jesus] was taken up by God unto Himself, not seeing death. (4.)

Muhammad Admits the Fact of the Crucifixion of Christ

And God said, "O Isa [Jesus], I will cause Thee to die, but I will take Thee up to Myself and deliver Thee from unbelievers!" (4.)

One God, Not Three Gods, According to the Scripture

O ye who have received the Scriptures, do not believe more than these sacred writings teach! Jesus, Son of Mary, was God's Apostle, His Word, a spirit proceeding from God. Do not say there are three gods--Allah, Isa, and Mary.[30]There is but one God, and He can have no son. (4.)

Forbidden Food

Ye are forbidden to eat that which dies of itself, blood, swine's flesh, and that on which the name of any other [pg 184]god than Allah has been invoked;[31] that which has beenstrangled, or killed by a blow, or by a fall, or what has been gored to death, and whatever has been sacrificed to idols. (5.)

Divination by Arrows Condemned

It is not allowed you to make division by casting lots with arrows.

Denial of the Divinity of Christ and the Trinity

Those are unbelievers who say that God is the Christ [lit., Messiah], Son of Mary. Nay, this Christ Himself said, "O Israelites, worship God, My Lord and yours!" He who associates with God any companion His equal shall be excluded from Paradise, and have his place in Hell fire. (5.)

Jesus Denies that He and His Mother were Gods

At the last day God will say unto Isa, "O Isa, Son of Mary, didst Thou say unto men, 'Take Me and My Mother for two Gods in addition to Allah'?" And He shall answer, "Praise be unto Thee. Thou knowest all things, and Thou knowest that I commanded men to worship Allah alone."

Footnotes

1. The deceased speaks constantly as if he were Osiris or some other god. This is supposed to give him the privileges and power of the god whose name he bears.

2. The Egyptians thought that in the lower world the heart or conscience was weighed, *i.e.*, judged.

3. This chapter and the like are found on stone, wood, porcelain, etc., figures, and attached to the mummy. It was supposed to act magically in transferring the tasks of the underworld from the person.

4. The storm-god, the arch-fiend of Ra, the sun-god

5. The suppliant has made a wax figure of Apepi, and, by sympathetic magic, imagines that by burning it he is destroying the power of the original. Such wax figures of the gods made for magical purposes were generally illegal.

6. There are many examples in the Book of the Dead of the magical potency attached to names. To invoke a god by his name was to control him.

7. The ass stands for Ra, the sun-god, and the eater of the ass is darkness or some eclipse, represented as one of the foes of Ra, in the vignette figured as a serpent on the back of an ass. Compare the Babylonian myth of Marduk and Tiamat.

8. The married name of Confucius.

9. Compare the method of Socrates in the investigation of truth.

10. In the above four "difficulties," note the reappearance of the law of reciprocity, the negative form of the Golden Rule.

11. A technical name for China, which was supposed to be enclosed by the four great oceans of the world. China is also called "The Middle Kingdom."

12. That is, those who have been invested with the sacred thread, which is a sign of having been initiated into the paternal caste. This ceremony takes place at the age of seven or nine years, but is only observed by the three higher castes. It is to be compared with the Christian rites of baptism and confirmation. Hindu boys, when invested with the sacred thread or cord, are said to be born again.

13. This spelling of the word ("Quran") represents the native Arabic pronunciation if it be remembered that "q" stands for a "k" sound proceeding from the lower part of the throat. The initial sound is therefore to be distinguished from that of the Arabic and Hebrew letters properly transliterated "k."

14. The pronunciation heard by the present writer among the Muslim Arabs of Egypt, Syria, etc. The word means literally "The Praised One" or "The One to be Praised." The "h," however, in the word is not the ordinary one, but that pronounced at the lower part of the throat, as the Arabic equivalent of "q" is. Hence this "h" is transliterated as "h" with a dot underneath it.

15. All the suras, except the ninth, begin with this formula, as, indeed, do most Arabic books, often even books of an immoral nature.

16. Muhammad's uncle, who, with his wife, rejected the prophet'» claims.

17. A word-play, Lahab meaning "flame."

18. Said by Muslim commentators to be one of the last ten nights of Ramadhan, the seventh of those nights reckoning backwards.

19. The earliest mention of the doctrine of abrogation of previous revelations. When Muhammad was convinced that what he had previously taught was erroneous he always professed to have received a new revelation annulling the earlier one bearing on the matter.

20. There is perhaps here an indirect reference to the alleged deification of the Virgin Mary by the Christians with whom Muhammad came in contact.

21. This is from one of the oldest suras. A most important Muslim tradition says that Muhammad declares this sura to be equal to a third of the rest of the Koran. Some say it represents the prophet's creed when he entered upon his mission.

22. This is directed against both the Mekkan belief that angels were daughters of God and also against the Christian doctrine that Jesus was the Son of God. Reference is also made, perhaps, to the Jewish description of Ezra as God's son.

23. Muhammad here adopts the Jewish and Arab myth that Solomon had a seal with the divine name (Yahwe) inscribed on it giving him control over winds and jinns, or demons.

24. In Arabic, Mary and Miriam are spelt exactly alike ("Miriam"). This evidently misled Muhammad. In sura 56 he describes the Virgin as a daughter of Amram, the father of Aaron, Moses, and Miriam. (See Numbers xxvi. 59, and Exodus xv. 20.)

25. This is a well-known Arab fable, based on a misunderstanding of I Kings iv. 33, influenced by the second Targum on Esther. See an English translation of this last in a commentary on Esther by Paul Cassel (T. & T. Clark), p. 263. This Targum is certainly older than the Koran, and it embodies Jewish legends of a still greater antiquity.

26. This legend about Mount Sinai is contained twice in the Jewish Talmud (Abodah Zarah Mishnah II, 2, and Shabbath Gemarah lxxxviii. 1). It is no doubt this Jewish tradition that suggested the above passage.

27. The point to which men turn in prayer, Zoroastrians pray towards the east--the direction of the rising sun; Jews towards Jerusalem, where the Temple was; and Muslims, from the utterance of this sura, towards Mekka. At first Muhammad adopted no Qiblah. On reaching Medinah, in order to conciliate the Jews he adopted Jerusalem as the Qiblah. But a year after reaching Medinah, he broke with the Jews and commanded his people to make the Kaabah their Qiblah.

28. The cube-like building in the centre of the mosque at Mekka, which contains the sacred black stone.

29. Ahmad and Muhammad have both the same meaning, *i.e.,* "the Praiseworthy One." Muslim commentators hold that the Paraclete (Comforter) promised in John xvi. 7 means Muhammad. In order to make this clear, however, they say we ought to read "Periklutos," *i.e.,* virtually Ahmad and Muhammad, instead of "Paracletos."

30. According to the Koran, Mary was worshipped as God by the Christians of Arabia.

31. According to sura 2, verse 174, the *Bismillah* (lit. "In the name of Allah," etc.) must be uttered before animals to be eaten are killed.

The End